# Mushrooms

# A Beginner's Guide To Home Cultivation

# Benjamin Hirst

## Copyright © 2015 Rach Helson LLC
### All rights reserved.

This document is geared towards providing exact and reliable information in regards to the topic and issue covered. The publication is sold with the idea that the publisher is not required to render accounting, officially permitted, or otherwise, qualified services. If advice is necessary, legal or professional, a practiced individual in the profession should be ordered.

From a Declaration of Principles which was accepted and approved equally by a Committee of the American Bar Association and a Committee of Publishers and Associations.

In no way is it legal to reproduce, duplicate, or transmit any part of this document in either electronic means or in printed format. Recording of this publication is strictly prohibited and any storage of this document is not allowed unless with written permission from the publisher. All rights reserved.

The information provided herein is stated to be truthful and consistent, in that any liability, in terms of inattention or otherwise, by any usage or abuse of any policies, processes, or directions contained within is the solitary and utter responsibility of the recipient reader. Under no circumstances will any legal responsibility or blame be held against the publisher for any reparation, damages, or monetary loss due to the information herein, either directly or indirectly.

Respective authors own all copyrights not held by the publisher.

The information herein is offered for informational purposes solely, and is universal as so. The presentation of the information is without contract or any type of guarantee assurance.

The trademarks that are used are without any consent, and the publication of the trademark is without permission or backing by the trademark owner. All trademarks, photographs, and brands within this book are for clarifying purposes only and are the owned by the owners themselves, not affiliated with this document.

# Table of Contents

**Introduction** . . . . . . . . . . . . . . . . . . . . . . . . . . . . . . . . 1
**Introduction to Mushrooms** . . . . . . . . . . . . . . . . . . . . . . . 3
    Mushrooms Are Not Plants, Vegetables or Animals . . . . . . . . . . . 3
    Mushroom Basics . . . . . . . . . . . . . . . . . . . . . . . . . . . . . 4
    How Does A Mushroom Grow? . . . . . . . . . . . . . . . . . . . . . 6
    Why Would People Want To Grow Mushrooms In The First Place? . . . 7
**An Overview Of Mushroom Cultivation** . . . . . . . . . . . . . . . . . 9
    Mushrooms And Ancient Man . . . . . . . . . . . . . . . . . . . . . . 9
    Modern Mushroom Cultivation . . . . . . . . . . . . . . . . . . . . . 11
    Mushrooms And You . . . . . . . . . . . . . . . . . . . . . . . . . . 12
**Health Benefits** . . . . . . . . . . . . . . . . . . . . . . . . . . . . . . 13
    Improves Metabolism . . . . . . . . . . . . . . . . . . . . . . . . . . 13
    The Only Food With Vitamin D . . . . . . . . . . . . . . . . . . . . 14
    Boosts The Immune System . . . . . . . . . . . . . . . . . . . . . . 14
    Serves As Antioxidants . . . . . . . . . . . . . . . . . . . . . . . . . 15
    Contains Selenium For Bladder Health . . . . . . . . . . . . . . . . 15
    Lowers The Risk Of Cancer, Diabetes, And Certain Heart Diseases . . . 15
    Anemia . . . . . . . . . . . . . . . . . . . . . . . . . . . . . . . . . . 16
    Cancer . . . . . . . . . . . . . . . . . . . . . . . . . . . . . . . . . . 16
    Diabetes . . . . . . . . . . . . . . . . . . . . . . . . . . . . . . . . . 16
    Heart Health . . . . . . . . . . . . . . . . . . . . . . . . . . . . . . . 17
    The Downside Of Mushrooms To Auto-Immune Diseases . . . . . . . 17
**Edible Mushrooms** . . . . . . . . . . . . . . . . . . . . . . . . . . . . 19
    Portobello Mushroom . . . . . . . . . . . . . . . . . . . . . . . . . . 19
    Oyster Mushroom . . . . . . . . . . . . . . . . . . . . . . . . . . . . 20
    Hen Of The Wood Mushroom . . . . . . . . . . . . . . . . . . . . . 20

Shiitake Mushroom . . . . . . . . . . . . . . . . . . . . . . 21
Crimini Mushroom . . . . . . . . . . . . . . . . . . . . . . 22
Chanterelle Mushrooms . . . . . . . . . . . . . . . . . . 22
White Button Mushroom . . . . . . . . . . . . . . . . . . 23
Porcini Mushroom . . . . . . . . . . . . . . . . . . . . . . 23
Enoki Mushroom . . . . . . . . . . . . . . . . . . . . . . . 24
Morel Mushroom . . . . . . . . . . . . . . . . . . . . . . . 24

**Medicinal Mushrooms** . . . . . . . . . . . . . . . . . . . . 25
Reishi Mushroom (Ganoderma lucidum) . . . . . . . . . . . . 25
Caterpillar Fungus (Cordyceps Sinensis) . . . . . . . . . . 26
God's Mushroom (Agaricus Blazei) . . . . . . . . . . . . . . 27
Chaga Mushroom (Inonotus Obliquus) . . . . . . . . . . . . . 27
Turkey Tail (Trametes Versicolor) . . . . . . . . . . . . . 28
Lion's Mane (Hericium Erinaceus) . . . . . . . . . . . . . . 29
Tinder Conk Mushroom (Fomes Fomentarius) . . . . . . . . . . 29
Chestnut Mushroom (Agrocybe Aegerita) . . . . . . . . . . . 30
Birch Bracket Mushroom (Piptoporus Betulinus) . . . . . . . 31
Cauliflower Mushroom (Sparassis Crispa) . . . . . . . . . . 32
Mesima (Phellinus Linteus) . . . . . . . . . . . . . . . . . 33

**Identifying Poisonous Mushrooms** . . . . . . . . . . . . . 35
Things To Know About Mushroom Poisoning: . . . . . . . . . . 36
Amanitas . . . . . . . . . . . . . . . . . . . . . . . . . . 37
Little Brown Mushrooms . . . . . . . . . . . . . . . . . . . 38
Big Laughing Jim . . . . . . . . . . . . . . . . . . . . . . 39
Big Red False Morel . . . . . . . . . . . . . . . . . . . . 39
Deadly Galerina . . . . . . . . . . . . . . . . . . . . . . 40
Destroying Angel . . . . . . . . . . . . . . . . . . . . . . 41
Emetic Russula . . . . . . . . . . . . . . . . . . . . . . . 41
False Morels . . . . . . . . . . . . . . . . . . . . . . . . 42
Green-Spored Lepiota . . . . . . . . . . . . . . . . . . . . 43

**Types Of Mushrooms You Can Grow** . . . . . . . . . . . . . . . . . . . 45
    Oyster Mushroom (Pleurotus Ostreatus) . . . . . . . . . . . . . . 45
    Shiitake (Lentinula Edodes) . . . . . . . . . . . . . . . . . . . . . . . . 46
    Button Mushrooms (Agaricus Bisporus) . . . . . . . . . . . . . . . 46
    Enokitake (Flammulina Velutipes) . . . . . . . . . . . . . . . . . . . 47
**Ready, Set, GROW!** . . . . . . . . . . . . . . . . . . . . . . . . . . . . . . . . 49
    Example One: Using a Commercially Available Mushroom Growing Kit. . . . . . . . . . . . . . . . . . . . . . . . . . . . . . . . . . . . . 54
    Example Two: Growing Mushrooms Indoors With Coffee Grounds. . . 55
    Getting Ready . . . . . . . . . . . . . . . . . . . . . . . . . . . . . . . . . . 56
    Example Three: Growing Mushrooms In Baking Pans. . . . . . . . . 57
    When You Are Ready, Gather Everything You Need And: . . . . . 57
    Example Four: Growing Mushroom In Logs. . . . . . . . . . . . . . 59
    Planting Dowels . . . . . . . . . . . . . . . . . . . . . . . . . . . . . . . . 60
    Growing Mushrooms Outdoors . . . . . . . . . . . . . . . . . . . . . 60
    Compost . . . . . . . . . . . . . . . . . . . . . . . . . . . . . . . . . . . . . 61
    Tips For Harvesting Your Mushrooms . . . . . . . . . . . . . . . . . 62
**Some Other Things You Need To Know About Growing Mushrooms.** . . . . . . . . . . . . . . . . . . . . . . . . . . . . . . . . . . . . . 63
    Why Grow Mushrooms? . . . . . . . . . . . . . . . . . . . . . . . . . 65
**Mushrooms Dishes** . . . . . . . . . . . . . . . . . . . . . . . . . . . . . . . 71
    Portobello Mushroom Sauté . . . . . . . . . . . . . . . . . . . . . . . 71
    Pho With Mushrooms. . . . . . . . . . . . . . . . . . . . . . . . . . . . 72
    Pappardelle With Wild Mushrooms. . . . . . . . . . . . . . . . . . 73
    Roasted Mushrooms With Butter And Wine . . . . . . . . . . . . 75
    Creamy Chanterelle Mushroom Soup . . . . . . . . . . . . . . . . 76
**Conclusion** . . . . . . . . . . . . . . . . . . . . . . . . . . . . . . . . . . . . . 79
**Other Related Books** . . . . . . . . . . . . . . . . . . . . . . . . . . . . . 81
**Photo Credits** . . . . . . . . . . . . . . . . . . . . . . . . . . . . . . . . . . 83

# Introduction

Thank you for purchasing, "Mushrooms: A Beginner's Guide To Home Cultivation." Most often, people think that growing mushrooms is a complicated and sensitive process. In this book, you'll find out just how easy it is to grow your own mushrooms safely and successfully indoors.

Growing mushrooms is fun, inexpensive and becoming more and more popular every day. It is my hope that the information in this book will provide you all you need to know, not only to grow edible mushrooms but also understand how they grow and why humans have been fascinated by them for so many thousands of years.

Welcome to the exciting world of the fungi kingdom!

Thanks again for purchasing this book, I hope you enjoy it!

Ben

*Mushrooms: A Beginner's guide To Home Cultivation*

# Introduction to Mushrooms

If you want to successfully grow your own mushrooms, it helps to have some idea of what they are and how they grow in nature first. This will help you understand why you are doing what you are doing when it comes time to start working with your mushrooms and growing materials.

While it's always a good idea to understand why you are doing something, it especially important in the case of growing mushrooms. Growing mushrooms isn't like growing other things. They operate by a different set of rules and have distinct needs that may be unfamiliar to someone who is used to gardening but not growing mushrooms.

You'll be sure to find growing mushrooms a fairly easy and straight forward process once a basic understanding of how they do what they do has been obtained, and you're comfortable with the vocabulary surrounding the subject.

## Mushrooms Are Not Plants, Vegetables or Animals

You may already know this as it is a rather common fact but mushrooms aren't technically plants. They are scientifically classified as fungi. Fungi are a bit of a puzzle to scientists and always have been. They aren't plants but share much in common with them.

They don't have a root system nor do fungi make chlorophyll, the chemical in plants that makes them green and able to transmute sunlight into food. Instead all fungi, including mushrooms, "eat" or more properly, absorb nutrients from what is nearby. They sustain themselves on the by-products of rotting vegetation, which is the reason they grow so well in damp, dark conditions.

If mushrooms are not plants, could they be animals? This questions is not as silly as it first seems, mushrooms occupy a place between plant and animal, as do all fungi. Because of this being sort of "in between" plant and animal fungi are classified as an entirely separate kingdom of organisms, which contains mushrooms, yeast, mold, and other countless variations of fungus.

## Mushroom Basics

A mushroom is a type of fungus, which consists of a spore-producing fruiting body ( often called the cap), which may or may not be atop a stem. Mushrooms always have what are called "gills" on the underside of the cap. The mushroom makes spores in the gills. Spores are how mushrooms reproduce. You can think of spores as seeds, they serve the same function but utilize an entirely different mechanism to achieve their goal of reproducing.

The study of mushrooms is called mycology and the growing them is technically referred to as "Fungiculture".

Mushrooms that grow in the wild tend to be found in damp, dark places. They are commonly found near decaying matter—either directly on a rotting log or tree or popping up out of the ground near a dead tree of decaying plant matter. It is possible for mushrooms to appear year round, depending on the type of mushrooms and your location. You are most likely to encounter mushrooms in the wild during the rainy cooler parts of spring, summer and fall.

When the conditions are right for mushrooms to appear, they do so quickly. It seems like they can burst out of nowhere sometimes, especially after a good rainstorm. Even though it sure looks to the eye that mushrooms just pop into existence, the reality is that they were growing there for several weeks already and just swelled up and expanded in size from absorbing rainwater. This process is similar to a dry sponge expanding when it gets wet and is just as magical.

# How Does A Mushroom Grow?

Every Mushroom starts about as a spore, which as we mentioned, functions as a seed. That is to say, a spore is a vehicle for reproduction just as a seed is. We also took note of the fact that this is about the only thing seeds and spores have in common.

When a mature mushroom releases spores, it does so by the thousands. These microscopic spores are caught by the wind and carried away from the parent mushroom.

When these newly released spores land on the ground and settle in, they begin to make what is called "Hyphae" which is analogous to a single root in a plant. It is a thin strand of fibrous material that the mushroom uses to pull nutrients out of the ground. These strands of Hyphae spread and entwine with each other in a way that is similar to a root system of a plant. This collected body of Hyphae is called the Mycelium.

It is tempting to call the Mycelium a root system, but it is not always underground and does not serve to stabilize the mushroom and keep it securely anchored in the dirt, the way a root system would. Mycelium resembles strands of pillow stuffing or cotton candy. The Mycelium of many mushrooms will entwine with each other, making sexual reproduction possible.

The stalks and caps eventually grow out of the Mycelium to produce the familiar image of a mushroom that we all know. These mushrooms then release their own spores, and the above process repeats itself.

When you grow mushrooms at home, you'll find yourself reproducing the environment that mushrooms enjoy in the wild. Namely, a dark, cool, damp spot with the proper type of rotting vegetation to feed the particular variety of mushroom that you are trying to grow.

The above information should provide you with a solid grasp of what mushrooms are and how they grow, which will enrich your growing experience in countless ways.

## Why Would People Want To Grow Mushrooms In The First Place?

There are many reasons for doing so. Over the course of human history, mushrooms have been used for food, medicine and in religious practices. Fungi in general and mushrooms, in particular, are capable of producing some interesting effects in the human body. These effects may come in the form of their nutritional value or their ability to cure illness and maintain vitality or even by facilitating the expansion of consciousness by inducing psychedelic experiences. Mushrooms are and have always been highly regarded by humans because they produce noticeable beneficial changes in the body and mind.

# An Overview Of Mushroom Cultivation

## Mushrooms And Ancient Man

It is believed that people have gathered and consumed mushrooms since the Stone Age. With little to no knowledge of what they were doing, early people discovered the effects different mushrooms could have on them by the simple process of trial and error.

This meant just eating any old mushroom they found laying about and waiting to see what happened. This is an incredibly dangerous and foolhardy way to go about it, but it was the only way available. Gathering wild mushrooms is still done today but is only recommended for experts in mushroom identification and not suitable at all for novices.

Many kinds of mushrooms are toxic to people, but only a few varieties are deadly. This doesn't mean that eating a poisonous mushroom is in any way an enjoyable experience–just a survivable one. Our ancient ancestors must have found enough benefit to eating mushrooms to keep up this dangerous method of trial and error for tens of thousands of years.

Eventually, early man learned enough about mushrooms to know that some are good; some are bad and that they can be cultivated, or grown on purpose. Purposeful mushroom growing probably started in Japan and China, both cultures that highly value mushrooms as food and medicine. It is estimated that the East was growing mushrooms long before the Egyptians, Greeks, and Romans discovered a reliable method for mushroom cultivation.

In the west, mushrooms were also popular. Egyptian hieroglyphs dating back almost five thousand years, depict people gathering mushrooms. The Egyptians considered the mushroom an important ingredient in their quest for immortality and it was a crime to eat them unless you were royalty.

The Greeks and Romans also held the mushroom in high regards, while there was no outright law forbidding anyone from eating mushrooms; they were very expensive and only available to those who could afford them.

To all these cultures, both east and west, the mushroom was always more than food. It was medicine as well. The medicinal nature of certain mushroom varieties was known to all of the ancient cultures. Chinese medical practices have made extensive use of mushrooms for centuries, and their use was a popular remedy for a variety of ailments.

In parts many parts of Central and South America and Northern Europe, psychoactive mushrooms were easily obtainable and it is easy to see the effect this had on the religious and spiritual practices of the cultures that had access to them. The spiritual effects of these mushrooms inspired entire religions and mysterious cults. The cultures that used them in this manner elevated the mushroom to the realm of the sacred and considered it a gift from the heavens. These mushrooms and the experiences they made available were something special to be cherished and revered. The use of psychoactive mushrooms is still popular today though they are mostly consumed in a recreational manner devoid of spiritual and religious overtones. It is also illegal in many countries to cultivate, possess or consume them.

## Modern Mushroom Cultivation

As you can see from the brief history of the relationship between humans and mushrooms, the human fascination with these fungal life forms is nearly as old as humans themselves. There has never been a culture where the use and cultivation of mushrooms weren't popular.

Modern interest in mushrooms dates back to the late 19th century when mushroom spores and reliable methods of cultivation were made available to the common person. Also around this time a book about growing mushrooms called "Mushrooms: How to Grow Them; A Practical Treatise on Mushroom Culture for Profit and Pleasure." was written by William Falconer, a Long Island Mushroom Grower.

The book, combined with the advances in technology that simplified the process of growing mushrooms paved the way for today's interest in small scale home mushroom cultivation.

## Mushrooms And You

Today, many people are becoming aware of all that mushrooms have to offer. The kinds of mushrooms that are commonly found in modern cooking are often highly nutritious and low in fat and calories. They contain minerals and other valuable compounds that are difficult to get in your diet from other foods.

Homegrown mushrooms are often better tasting and pack a higher nutritional punch than their store bought counterparts. It is also cheaper to grow them yourself. One of the main reasons people try their hand at growing mushrooms is to save money. While they are no longer as prohibitively expensive as they were in the ancient world, they still can run you a pretty penny.

Growing mushrooms is also pursued as a hobby because it is enjoyable and allows the cultivator a glimpse into the strange world of the fungi kingdom. It allows you to share the same sense of awe and wonder our ancestors had when they first encountered with mushrooms.

If you're a fan of culinary mushrooms, growing your own will provide you with an abundance of them while saving you money.

# Health Benefits

Who says that fungus cannot do any good to your health? Mushrooms, though sometimes considered as vegetables are not really plants but fungi. What's interesting to note is that mushrooms are actually nutritious, too. In fact, they are called "functional foods" because they are low in all of those substances that the body does not need much of; fat, cholesterol, calories, and sodium.

For example, a cup of raw white mushrooms has a total of 15 calories, 2.2 grams of protein, 2.3 grams of carbohydrates and has 0 grams of fat. And though mushrooms come in different varieties, they pretty much have the same amount of nutrients per serving.

## Improves Metabolism

Mushrooms are high in B vitamins like *thiamine* (B1), *riboflavin* (B2), *niacin* (B3), *pantothenic acid* (B5), and *folate* (B9). These B vitamins promote a healthy metabolism and lessen the risk of stroke. *Thiamine* is responsible for the production of new and healthy cells. It is often called the anti-stress vitamin because of its capability to fortify the immune system. *Riboflavin* is an antioxidant that helps the body in fighting free radicals or those particles in the body that cause damage to cells. This B vitamin slows the aging process and reduces the risk of heart disease. *Niacin* is known for boosting high-density lipoprotein (HDL) or the good cholesterol, which balances the bad cholesterol in the blood. *Pantothenic acid*, which is present in almost all food groups, is the vitamin responsible for the conversion of fats and carbohydrates into energy. Lastly, *folate* or *folic acid* is linked to having a good memory. It's also the vitamin responsible for the development of the fetus.

B Vitamins are responsible for promoting a better metabolism. This is because these vitamins help in the conversion of carbohydrates into glucose, which the body then burns to produce energy. Another role of B vitamins is metabolizing fats and proteins.

## The Only Food With Vitamin D

Mushrooms are a good source of vitamin D. In fact, it's the only food that contains this critical vitamin. Humans stay under the sun to get vitamin D, and that's also what happens to mushrooms as they are exposed to sunlight. As a matter of fact, when mushrooms are exposed to ultraviolet B, that's when their sterol ergosterol is converted to vitamin D.

## Boosts The Immune System

According to studies published by the American Society for Nutrition, mushrooms, particularly white button mushrooms, increases antiviral substances and other proteins that the cell releases when repairing and protecting the body. It also promotes the ripening of the dendritic cells found in the bone marrow, thus raising the defense against microbes that enters the body.

## Serves As Antioxidants

Antioxidants are free radical fighting agents of the body. They help the body against dangerous oxygen molecules called free radicals. Antioxidants are mostly found among colorful vegetables but according to research, mushrooms like Portobello and crimini has the same oxygen radical absorbance capacity as that of a red pepper. White bottom mushrooms, on the other hand, were found to have a greater amount of antioxidants than that of tomatoes, carrots, zucchini, green peppers, or pumpkins. Antioxidants are linked to the prevention of cancer, heart diseases, and even Alzheimer's.

## Contains Selenium For Bladder Health

Selenium is a rare mineral to find in one's diet but according to researchers, mushrooms are loaded with selenium, which is vital for bladder health. In fact, crimini mushrooms are an excellent source of selenium, 100 grams of raw crimini makes up 47 percent of your daily needs. Based on a published study in *Cancer Epidemiology, Biomarkers & Prevention*, a high level of selenium has a great impact on lowering the risk of bladder cancer. Selenium is also noted for improved immunity response to infections, enhances fertility among women, as well as reduces the risk of cancer and thyroid diseases.

## Lowers The Risk Of Cancer, Diabetes, And Certain Heart Diseases

It's not only in consuming vegetables and fruits that we can prevent the development of dreaded diseases. A lot of studies have been made and proved that organically grown mushrooms, too can help lower the risk of obesity, diabetes, heart diseases, and cancer. It even helps nourish the hair and skin, as well as promote good weight management.

## Anemia

People suffering from anemia are characterized by having very low levels of iron in their blood. This results in fatigue, headache, digestive problems and even reduced neural functions. Mushrooms are a cheap source of iron, which helps in maintaining a healthy formation of red blood cells in the body.

## Cancer

Mushrooms contain compounds like lectins, glucans, proteins, and carbohydrates, which inhibits the development of cancer. According to research, daily intake of mushrooms can help prevent the possibility of breast cancers up to 60% among women. In another research, it has been found that mushrooms contain enzyme 5 alpha reductase that is linked to the prevention of prostate cancer among men.

## Diabetes

Fiber diet among people with diabetes is vital. Fiber-rich diets can help type 1 diabetics to lower their glucose levels. The same diet can also improve type 2 diabetics to maintain good blood sugar, lipids, and insulin levels. This dietary fiber can be obtained from mushrooms. In fact, just a cup of grilled portabella mushroom or a cup of stir-fried shiitake has about 3 grams of fiber.

## Heart Health

Mushrooms are also rich in potassium and vitamin C, which helps in improving the cardiovascular health. Blood pressure is regulated by the teamwork between potassium and sodium. Adding mushrooms to your diet will help you lower your cholesterol level, improve your blood pressure, and prevent you from any cardiovascular disease.

## The Downside Of Mushrooms To Auto-Immune Diseases

Beta glucans are sugars found in the cell walls of mushrooms. They are naturally good for most people. In fact, they are helpful for boosting the immune system as well as for the prevention of some diseases. But it can also be a risk for people with autoimmune conditions like lupus, multiple sclerosis, asthma, and rheumatoid arthritis. What's yet to find out is whether the negative effect would apply only for large amounts of beta-glucan intake among people suffering from the said conditions.

# Edible Mushrooms

Mushrooms are not just delicious but healthy as well. However, some of those gourmet varieties are either hard to find fresh or are too expensive for one to afford. If you are planning to grow your own mushrooms, you may want to consider the following mushrooms, which you can include in your dishes:

## Portobello Mushroom

The Portobello mushroom (*Agaricus bisporus*) which is sometimes called, Portabella, open cap, or field mushroom is home to Italian cooking. It is native to the grasslands of North America and Europe. These mushrooms are white when immature and are called criminis, common mushrooms, or white mushrooms. It's when it matures and turns to a brownish color that it's called Portobello mushroom.

Portobello mushrooms are rich in flavor and are commonly cooked in sauces and pasta. They are considered a great meat substitute. You can also enjoy Portobello's large caps grilled and marinated.

## Oyster Mushroom

The Oyster mushroom (Pleurotus) is a gilled mushroom. The word Pleurotus is actually a Greek word meaning "side ear." Other names that it is known for are tree oyster, pleurotte en huître, shimeji, angel's wings, or abalone mushroom.

Oyster mushrooms are one of the most widely eaten types of mushroom. This type of mushroom is common among tropical and temperate climates. They are commonly found growing on tree's sides.

Oyster mushrooms are mostly used in Chinese and Japanese cooking and are usually stir-fried or are included in soups.

## Hen Of The Wood Mushroom

The Hen of the Wood mushroom (*Grifola frondosa*) is also called ram's head, or sheep's head because of its soft, feathery look. In Japan, they are known as Maitake, which actually means dancing mushrooms. When not cultivated, hen of the woods naturally grows in the woods. They are noted for their earthy aroma and meaty flavor.

Hen of the Wood is used as meat substitute. They are also perfect for noodle dishes and for grilling.

## Shiitake Mushroom

The Shiitake is known for a lot of other names such as black winter, black forest, black mushroom, brown oak, forest mushroom, golden oak, Chinese black, and Donko. The word shiitake is a Japanese word meaning "oak fungus" because it's among oaks that this mushroom is usually found in the wild. This mushroom is one of the most cultivated types of mushroom and is famed for its caps, which are slightly curled.

Shiitake mushrooms can be enjoyed fresh or dried. They give a light woodsy flavor and are usually used in sautéing for enhanced flavor or can be added to soups.

## Crimini Mushroom

Crimini mushrooms (*Basidiomycotina*) are brown cap mushrooms, which come in light tan colors to rich brown. They are noted for their earthy and intense flavor and are usually used as a substitute for button mushrooms for a more full-bodied taste.

Crimini mushrooms are actually young portobellos and are otherwise known as baby bellas, Italian brown, golden Italian, or Cremini.

## Chanterelle Mushrooms

Chanterelle mushrooms are vase-shaped mushrooms usually ranging from a bright yellow color to orange. They are otherwise known as girolle or egg mushroom. These mushrooms give a nutty and delicate flavor. They are really expensive when fresh and can also be bought canned or dried. Chanterelle mushrooms are the most known among wild mushrooms because they are not too easy to cultivate.

Chanterelle mushrooms are usually added late in dishes as cooking them for a longer period to avoid toughening. Chanterelle mushrooms are common among European cuisines. They are usually used in risottos, sauces, as well as salads.

## White Button Mushroom

The White button mushroom or table mushroom has a lighter taste than its counterparts (Crimini and Portobello mushrooms). In French, these mushrooms are called champignons. White button mushrooms are easy to grow and are can be found almost everywhere in the United States. They are enjoyed raw or cooked. White button mushrooms are popular in soups, pizzas, and salads.

## Porcini Mushroom

The Porcini mushroom or porcini comes from the Italian word which means "piglets." This mushroom is also called cèpe, Steinpilz, or king bolete. Porcini mushrooms can grow up to about 12 inches in diameter and can weigh up to 1 kilogram when mature. They are brown or reddish brown and have a sticky texture. They have a rather thick stem and are the kind of mushrooms that resembles the traditional fairytale toadstool.

Porcini mushrooms have a lot of cooking uses including pasta, soups, and sauces. They are also used as a meat substitute. They give a pungent flavor and are very expensive in the market. They are famous in Italy but are also grown in Europe, North America, South Africa, and New Zealand.

## Enoki Mushroom

The Enoki mushroom is also known as enokitake, snow puff, golden mushrooms, or velvet stem. These mushrooms have long stems and small snow-white caps. Little white mushrooms are connected at its base and look similar to that of bean sprouts. Enoki mushrooms are light and give an almost fruity flavor with a slight crunch.

Enoki mushrooms are enjoyed fresh or cooked. They are common among Asian cuisine and are best for salads, sandwiches, pasta, and soups.

## Morel Mushroom

The Morel mushroom is also called black morel and is kin to the highly prized truffle. Its color ranges from tan to dark brown. They are spongy, cone-shaped mushrooms which are usually common during the spring.

Morel mushrooms give a woodsy and earthy aroma and a nutty flavor. They are expensive in the market and can be used fresh, canned, or dried.

# Medicinal Mushrooms

The Chinese and Egyptians were the first people to discover the medicinal value of mushrooms. The Egyptians looked at mushrooms with so much appreciation that they even linked mushrooms to immortality. As a matter of fact, they included mushrooms in the early diet of the Pharaohs to wish them a longer life. The Chinese, on the other hand, included mushrooms in their diet because they related mushrooms to longevity.

Here are some of the mushrooms, that are known for their medicinal value:

## Reishi Mushroom (Ganoderma lucidum)

The Reishi mushroom is soft when fresh. It has no gills under its kidney-shaped cap, which is red varnish in color. Reishi mushrooms are classified as a polypore because it releases spores through some fine pores. Reishi mushrooms come in six varieties: (1) Red Reishi also called *Akashiba*; (2) Black Reishi or *Kuroshiba*; (3) Blue Reishi called *Aoshiba*; (4) Yellow Reishi known as *Kishiba*; (5) White Reishi or *Shiroshiba*; and (6) the Purple Reishi called *Murasakishiba*.

Each reishi variety supports the human body in a unique way. The red one is said to be good for the heart. The green mushroom ensures liver health. The yellow one is aimed to take care of the spleen. The white mushroom is good for the lungs. The black one is great for kidney health. And the purple mushroom is helpful for boosting essence (*jing*).

According to scientific studies, The Reishi mushroom showed properties significant to the healing of tumors. This mushroom is also noted for its help in maintaining normal blood sugar and cholesterol levels.

## Caterpillar Fungus (Cordyceps Sinensis)

Caterpillar Fungus belongs to the family of ascomycete fungi or sac fungi. Its name comes from the Latin '*cord*' which means club and '*ceps*' which means head. This mushroom is entomopathogenic because it gets its nutrients by attacking caterpillars and other insects and arthropods.

Cordyceps is helpful in controlling the blood sugar level from dropping below an acceptable level. It also contains properties that catalyze the anti-depressant performance in the body. It is also a good antibacterial fungi, that is why it is noted to be helpful for Hepatitis B patients. It contains antiviral properties that suppress pneumococcal viruses, golden staph, and herpes viruses as well. Furthermore, this mushroom enhances the body's natural way of detoxification.

Research also shows that the Cordyceps mushroom has a lot of potential in treating even dreaded diseases like cancer and oncologists worldwide have been recommending the use of this mushroom as a conventional way to fight cancer. More so, patients undergoing chemotherapy and radiation treatments can use this mushroom to give their body a fresh boost of energy. Caterpillar mushrooms help treat insulin problems, soothe the nervous system to reduce anxiety levels, and fight respiratory diseases. To put it simply, this mushroom helps keep the body holistic.

## God's Mushroom (Agaricus Blazei)

Unlike other mushrooms, this one was first identified in the West, somewhere in the northeastern part of the US and Canada. Agaricus blazei is a capped mushroom. Its cap varies from white, gray, and reddish brown. It is composed of silk-like fibers on the surface, which grows into tiny scales.

God's mushroom has properties known to improve body immunity and fight infections and certain cancers. Other studies also showed that this mushroom helps improve and lower blood cholesterol, hampers the negative effects of pathogens in the body, as well as prevents angiogenesis.

God's mushrooms are a rich mushroom. It contains 40-45% protein, 38-45% carbohydrates, 6-8% fiber, and 3-4% fats. It's also loaded with B vitamins. Because of its rich composition it is also noted for relieving physical and mental stresses, reducing the development of osteoporosis and for relieving gastric ulcers.

## Chaga Mushroom (Inonotus Obliquus)

The Chaga mushroom usually grows in cold places and is commonly found dwelling on Birch trees. It belongs to the family of Hymenochaetaceae. This mushroom is very popular among countries like Russia and Korea, as well as the Northern and Eastern Europe. It is a black mushroom because it contains a high level of melanin, which gives it a dark color pigment.

Wild Chaga mushrooms are noted for their anti-tumor properties. Scientists in Russia and Finland have also found out that this mushroom has properties that can fight cancers like gastric, breast, liver, and uterine cancers. This mushroom is also traditionally used to treat psoriasis, a skin condition that is characterized by having rough red patches. The Chaga mushroom is valued for its medicinal qualities as far back as the 16$^{th}$ century. It is famed for its role in the treatment of gastritis and tuberculosis.

## Turkey Tail (Trametes Versicolor)

Turkey tail, or Trametes versicolor, is another polypore mushroom. It grows almost anywhere. It is known as Turkey tail because of its variation of colors that are similar to that of the turkey's tail. This mushroom has been used as medicine in China and Japan for a long time.

The Turkey tail has proven its worth in the medicine world. In fact, the cancer drug called polysaccharide-K (Kresin) is derived from this mushroom. Kresin is noted as a medicine used together with chemotherapy when treating patients with cancer. Another role of this drug is to minimize the negative impact of drugs used during chemotherapy. Among cancer types, Kresin is best recommended for colorectal and stomach cancer sufferers. Aside from the treatment of cancer, turkey tail is also useful for other diseases like hepatitis B and Malaria.

## Lion's Mane (Hericium Erinaceus)

Lion's Mane is also called the Hedgehog Mushroom, Satyr's Beard, or Bearded Tooth Mushroom. It was first discovered in the Northern America. This mushroom is abundant during the summer and it naturally grows on hardwoods like the American beech trees.

Lion's Mane was used by the Chinese as far back as 2000 B.C. It is found to contain substances like palmitic acid, threitol, and D-arabinitol, which play a vital role in the regulation of blood sugar and lipid levels in the blood. Aside from these substances, Lion's Mane is also noted for its antioxidant properties.

According to studies, Lion's Mane is also beneficial to suppress inflammation and ulcers. It is also used as a treatment for pancreatitis, Crohn's disease, hemorrhoids, and osteoporosis. Lion's Mane is also used by patients undergoing chemotherapy as it reduces the horrible side effects of the procedure and reduces fatigue and nausea.

## Tinder Conk Mushroom (Fomes Fomentarius)

The Tinder Conk Mushroom is considered a fungal plant pathogen. It is known by other names like Tinder Polypore, Hoof Fungus, Tinder fungus, and Ice Man. Its body is like that of horse hoofs and varies in color from silvery gray to black. This mushroom grows on tree barks as a parasite and when the tree eventually dies, it stays in the bark and acts as a decomposer. Tinder Conk comes with a fruity smell but is not considered edible because of its acrid taste.

Tinder Conk contains an ingredient called Amadou. This substance is valuable for drying teeth. It is also used by surgeons to stop bleeding during surgery. As a polypore, Tinder Conk is known for other medicinal benefits. During the 5$^{th}$ century B.C., it was used for the cauterization of wounds. It is also used in Europe as a cure for hemorrhoids, dysmenorrhea, and bladder disorders. While in India, Tinder Conk is used primarily as a diuretic, a laxative, as well as remedy for steadying the nerves. In China, it is known for its work in treating throat, uterus, and stomach cancers.

## Chestnut Mushroom (Agrocybe Aegerita)

The Chestnut mushroom looks like a darker version of the button mushroom, but it actually belongs in the category of white rot fungi. It has gills that range from pink to a darkish brown color, that's why it is sometimes called the 'brown cap mushroom.' Chestnut mushrooms come in about 100 varying species, some of them poisonous. And because there is a very little difference in physical appearance, only the more experienced people with this type of mushroom are able to identify the species, which are edible.

Chestnut Mushroom cultivation began with the Greeks and Romans. According to myth, this mushroom came as a result of a lightning struck. Today, this mushroom is widely cultivated in Korea, China, Australia, and Japan.

The Chestnut Mushroom is used by the Chinese for stomach treatments. It helps keeps the spleen and the kidneys nourished and working well. Today, this mushroom is identified for its anti-inflammatory, antifungal, antitumor, and antibiotic properties. It has compounds containing prohibitive properties against cyclooxygenase enzyme. Aside from that, The Chestnut Mushroom is also noted for its anti-cancer properties. It's also used to slow down the development of osteoporosis.

## Birch Bracket Mushroom (Piptoporus Betulinus)

The Birch Bracket Mushroom, otherwise known as Razor Strop or Birch Polypore is classified as saprophytic fungi belonging to the family of Fomitopsidaceae. It is usually found dwelling on birch trees. A Birch Bracket Mushroom's lifespan can extend beyond twelve months. In fact, it was found inside of a mummy that was discovered in 1991.

The Birch Bracket Mushroom is used as medicine in different parts of the world. During the old times, it was used as a medicine to clear stomach and digestive parasites by using it as a laxative added to tea. It is also noted that tea brewed together with this mushroom is great for soothing the nerves and relieving fatigue.

One of the medicinal benefits of this mushroom is in boosting the immune system. It is also noted for its antiseptic properties and is used as a bandage to fight wound infections. People who use it as antiseptic confirm that it not only helps heal the wounds fast but also prevents the appearance of scars.

Another role of the Birch Bracket Mushroom is as anti-inflammatory. It helps numb pain without affecting the Central Nervous System. This is one of the reasons that this mushroom is valued even over synthetic medicine.

According to a study, Birch Bracket Mushroom was found to contain ketones, terpenes, aldehydes, and aliphatic alcohol. It also has polyporenic acids which are an anti-inflammatory substance.

## Cauliflower Mushroom (Sparassis Crispa)

The Cauliflower Mushroom is classified both as parasitic and saprophytic. It looks similar to that of the cauliflower head. Hence, it is called Cauliflower Mushroom. Others say that it looks like a brain and have coined it Brain fungus. Other names that this mushroom is called are Hen of the woods, Ruffle Mushroom, White Fungus, and Hanabiratake.

The Cauliflower Mushroom grows around conifer trees and pine trees. It grows in temperate areas and is widely cultivated by farmers in Australia, Japan, Korea and the US.

In scientific studies done on mice, it was discovered that the Cauliflower mushroom contains substances that raise the body's hemoglobin level, which eventually help boost the immune system, making sure that the red blood cells in the body are healthy. Cauliflower Mushrooms are also known for their anti-tumor properties. In a study done on mice, it was used to successfully fight Sarcoma 180 which is the tumor affecting the tissues of mice.

In a different study, it was also discovered that Cauliflower Mushroom contains anti-fungal properties. It has the ability to counter various fungal infections that can be as serious as those that reach the internal organs and spread throughout the body.

## Mesima (Phellinus Linteus)

Mesima is a mushroom that looks similarly to that of a hoof. It comes in colors varying from dark brown to black. This mushroom is commonly found in countries like China, Japan, and Korea. Mesima naturally grows on the branches and stems of mulberry trees. In China, this mushroom is called Song-Gen. In Korea, it's called Sang-Hwang. And in Japan, it is known as Mesimakobu.

Mesima is made into a tea and drank on a regular basis in Korea to boost the immune system like a vitamin. This mushroom is known in Asian countries as medicine to relieve diarrhea, cancers, and other gastroenteric problems. This mushroom is rich in Beta D-gluten and Lectin, which are substances that help strengthen the body's immunity.

Mesima is also best for regulating the blood sugar level because of the presence of interfungins. Because of this, Mesima is highly recommended for Type 2 diabetes patients. Adding this mushroom in their diet has been known to help. Another great medicinal benefit that Mesima is known for is in the treatment of hemorrhages. It was also linked to the possible treatment of hemophilia.

# Identifying Poisonous Mushrooms

Not all mushrooms are beneficial for us. There are also many types of mushrooms that are poisonous. Mycetism or mushroom poisoning is the term used when referring to the harmful effects due to the ingestion of the toxins present in mushrooms. And this may range from a simple gastrointestinal discomfort or may even cause death.

One of the most common causes of mushroom poisoning is that people misidentify poisonous ones as edible because of their close resemblance. That is why it is very vital for would-be mushroom farmers to be very familiar with the mushrooms that they would like to plant and go as far as learning their slight differences with the toxic species that look like them.

Folk traditions have listed certain rules for identifying when a particular mushroom is poisonous or safe. However, even mushroom experts will tell you that there are no generic rules for identifying poisonous mushrooms. Here are some of those folklore rules:

1. Brightly colored mushrooms are poisonous.
2. Animals and insects will naturally avoid toxic mushrooms.
3. Poisonous mushrooms can blacken silver.

4. Poisonous mushrooms normally taste bad.
5. All mushrooms are safe once cooked. (folklore, not to be trusted, always consult an expert)
6. When boiled together with rice, a poisonous mushroom will turn the rice to red.
7. Poisonous mushrooms have a pointed cap.

## Things To Know About Mushroom Poisoning:

1. The symptoms of mushroom poisoning may not show immediately. Sometimes, the symptoms can be delayed for up to 12 hours or longer.
2. There are instances when, after ingesting a poisonous mushroom, the symptoms seem to go away. However, the toxin will remain in your system for days.
3. Handling a poisonous mushroom may not be much of a hazard to your health, let's say when taking specimen samples. However, you can contaminate other mushrooms if you place them all in the same container. When keeping different species of mushrooms, it's best to keep them wrapped separately if you are storing them in the same basket or container, or better yet, just keep them in separate containers.
4. Even edible mushrooms may cause allergic reactions, especially to those that are highly

sensitive. Make sure to take only a few small bites if it's your first time eating any kind of mushroom.

5. Since most cases of mushroom poisoning among immigrants and foreigners happen due to mistaking a poisonous one with a similarly looking edible mushroom they have back home, it's best to use local references to identify the mushroom's local species.

6. Mushrooms' common names are sometimes confusing because one mushroom may have up to 4 or 5 other common names. Try learning the Latin names for accuracy purposes.

7. Mushroom poisoning has no antidotes. What doctors normally do is just treat whatever damage the toxins may have done to the body.

Instead of gambling with your safety by following folklore rules, it would be better that we familiarize ourselves with some of the most noted poisonous mushrooms. Here are a couple of samples of poisonous mushrooms:

## Amanitas

The Amanita is often mistaken for the edible shaggy mane mushroom or Coprinus comatus, especially when still immature. The Amanita species has been known to be the cause of about 90% of mushroom-related deaths.

The Amanita resembles an egg-shaped button that looks like a small puffball when immature. As it grows, it breaks open and eventually develops into a gilled mushroom with caps that looks like a parasol. The cap may be red, brown, yellow or white in color. The Amanita also has a cup that looks like a sac at the base of the stem, which is usually buried in the soil, a ring on its stem, a white gill, and a white spore print.

Amanita species naturally grow in woodland grounds and are abundant during summer and fall seasons. This mushroom is usually found among rotting logs.

Amanitas contain a substance called amanitin, which is known to be one of the most lethal poisons found in nature. In fact, ingesting just the mushroom cap can lead to death. It also contains amatoxins, which destroy the liver. Some of the other species belonging to The Amanita is Amanita phalloides or destroying angels, of which the subspecies Amanita virosa, Amanita bisporigera, and Amanita ocreata are part of.

## Little Brown Mushrooms

Little brown mushrooms come from the family of capped mushrooms in the phylum Basidiomycota. This mushroom category is composed of hundreds of different species ranging from small to medium-sized mushrooms. They also come in a range of colors, from brown to tan with the cap and well-defined stalk that most mushrooms have. Even mushroom experts are having a difficulty sorting little brown mushrooms into species, of which most are poisonous.

Little brown mushrooms thrive in summer, spring, and fall in almost any kind of habitat. They grow well on wood, in the soil, in lawns, forests, and pasture lands. There are some little brown mushrooms that are harmless but because they come in such a wide variety, it would be best to avoid all of them. Some species of this mushroom are mildly poisonous, some hallucinogenic, and still others, lethal.

## Big Laughing Jim

Big Laughing Jim is from the family Cortinariaceae. This mushroom is described as a big orange-yellow mushroom with a ring on its stalk. It also grows in clusters among trunks and tree stumps from August to October. This mushroom usually grows as a network of mycelium on rotting logs, and tree roots. Its cap usually ranges in color from orange to fawn. It also has tiny smooth scales. Its gills and spore print are normally yellow or rust and the spacing of the gills are rather crowded. It smells similar to anise and has a bitter taste.

Big Laughing Jim looks similar to the Honey Mushroom or Armillaria mellea and the Ringless Honey Mushroom or the Armillaria tabescens. It has also been compared to that of the Jack-o'lantern (Omphalotus illudens) and the deadly galerina (Galerina autumnalis).

Big Laughing Jim species are poisonous. Though some stories circulate that there are instances of experiencing only mild hallucinogenic effects, that occurrence very rarely happens.

## Big Red False Morel

Big Red False Morel (Gyromitra caroliniana) is from the family Discinaceae. It's a reddish brown brain-like cap that has a white stalk with cottony tissue. It is similar to Gabled false morel (Gyromitra brunnea) and true morels (Morchella spp.)

The Big Red False Morel is usually around during the months of March to May. It grows in groups in mixed woods. Its cap grows from 1 ½ to 7 inches and can grow to about 10 inches in height. This mushroom is potentially deadly. Although some people from Missouri that accidentally ate false morels did not have any ill effects afterward, there are people that have suffered serious illnesses and those who have died.

## Deadly Galerina

Deadly galerina comes from the family Hymenogastraceae. This mushroom has a sticky brown cap, a gill that ranges from yellow to rush and has a ring on its stalk. Some of the mushrooms that look similar to deadly galerina are velvet foot (Flammulina velutipes), honey mushroom (Armillaria mellea), and ringless honey mushroom (A. tabescens).

Deadly galerina grows along coniferous logs and often are scattered or clustered. It is abundant all year round, especially during the months of September to November.

This mushroom contains amatoxins, which is naturally accumulated in the liver cells. Amatoxins disrupt the function of the liver. It also attacks the kidneys. Once ingested, amatoxins may result in severe abdominal pain, diarrhea, and vomiting lasting from six to nine hours. More severe effects may affect the liver and result in gastrointestinal bleeding, and even coma. Some have been known to suffer from kidney failure and even death within seven days of consumption.

## Destroying Angel

Destroying Angel is a group of closely related deadly all-white mushrooms from genus Amanita. It comes from the family Amanitaceae. Aside from being an all-white mushroom, it is also noted for its ring on its stalk. It also has a large saclike cup around its base. Destroying angels are naturally found in the woods and grasses, usually near trees. They are abundant during the months of June to November.

It's cap has a central swelling and a smooth margin which is shiny white, and it gets tacky when wet. Its gills are narrow to broad and have a close spacing. Its stalk is sometimes enlarged at the base and has a cottony texture. Its spores, when magnified, are smooth and are almost round to round. Destroying angels are often mistaken for meadow mushrooms except for the latter's gills, which turn brown.

Destroying Angel is a deserving name because of its toxicity level. Some symptoms of destroying angel poisoning are vomiting, cramps, and diarrhea which appear 6-24 hours after ingestion. It hits the kidney and liver and may eventually cause death. Even livestock and pets are not exempt from the toxin that this mushroom contains.

## Emetic Russula

Emetic Russula also called Russula emetic is sometimes referred to as "the sickener". It is a basidiomycete mushroom. It comes from the family Russulaceae. It has a red cap that has off-white gills and stalk. Both the flesh and stalk of this mushroom are brittle. Emetic Russula may grow singly or in groups. They are often found in the woods growing in mosses. They are abundant during the months of July to October.

The Emetic Russula's cap is usually cushion-shaped to vase-shaped, with an incurved margin, and is smooth yet sticky. The gills are broad and attached. The stalk is straight and slightly enlarges at the base. It is off-white in color and has a wrinkled texture. The spores of the Emetic Russula, when magnified, are elliptical to oval. Most russulas look alike. They come in a lot of varieties, and a lot of them are red. That's why it's hard to tell one from the other.

Emetic Russula is considered poisonous. One of the symptoms of ingesting this mushroom is vomiting. Hence, it is also called vomiting russula. It tastes very spicy, acrid and hot at the same time. Other symptoms attached to the sickener are nausea, abdominal cramps, and diarrhea, which may appear a half hour after ingesting the poisonous mushroom.

## False Morels

False Morels come from the family that falls under phylum Ascomycota or sac fungi. It is likened to the true morels of the genus Morchella, that is why it is called a False Morel. And similar to Morchella, False Morel also belongs to the Pezizales. However, that group is subdivided into several groups into three families: Morchellaceae, Discinaceae, and Helvellaceae.

Identifying Poisonous Mushrooms:

False morels are mushrooms with wrinkled and irregular caps, which are often described as saddle-shaped or brain-like. They come in colors ranging from black, gray, brown, white, and red. One False Morsel species called the bid red false morel, or Gyromitra caroliniana, is known for its reddish cap. It's also called the elephant ears, brain mushrooms, and Arkansas morels. False morels are abundant during spring, fall, and summer in the woodland grounds.

Up to now, labeling False Morel as a poisonous mushroom is still under debate. This is because the mushroom is considered edible, however, deadly when eaten fresh. On some researches done, there are findings that the toxins inside the body remains even after proper treatment.

## Green-Spored Lepiota

Green-Spored Lepiota is a large white mushroom. It has cream-colored scales. Its gills are white that turn a grayish green color. It also has a stalk ring. Its cap grows to a width of up to 12 inches. Its stalk can grow up to 10 inches in height. Its stalk width can grow up to an inch in width.

This mushroom grows abundantly during the months of July to September. Some of the other mushrooms that it resembles are the Reddening lepiota (Leucoagaricus americanus), Parasol (Macrolepiota procera), The Amanita and Shaggy mane (Cornipus comatus).

The Green-Spored Lepiota is usually found in summer and fall among meadows, pasturelands, and lawns. This mushrooms often shows itself in fairy rings and emerges as a circle of mushrooms.

# Types Of Mushrooms You Can Grow

Your success as a small-scale mushroom cultivator largely hinges on which variety of mushroom you choose to grow. Mushrooms are a lot like people; some are easier to deal with than others. As a beginner, your focus should be on learning the growing process and becoming familiar with it. This means choosing a variety that has consistently proven itself to respond well to indoor growing.

## Oyster Mushroom (Pleurotus Ostreatus)

This is the number one choice for home mushroom growing, especially to those new to the hobby. Oyster mushrooms are among the easiest type of mushroom to grow on a small scale and the most popular choice for use with a commercially available mushroom growing kit. Because of how easy they are to cultivate and their high yield and success rate, it will be assumed that you are growing Oyster mushrooms when we discuss different growing methods in the next chapter.

You are highly encouraged to select this variety for your maiden voyage into home mushroom cultivation.

Oyster mushrooms have no stalks and resemble an ear. In fact, the scientific name for oyster mushrooms comes from the Greek word for "Ear". In the wild, they grow on the sides of trees.

## Shiitake (Lentinula Edodes)

Shiitake mushrooms are one of the most popular varieties of mushroom available today and account for nearly twenty-five percent of the total amount of cultivated mushrooms annually. In the past, these mushrooms were very rare and expensive due to the long time they take to grow. In the wild, these mushrooms are found growing on rotting logs. It can take several years for the mushroom to reach the stage where it is ready to be harvested. It was also difficult to get this variety to grow in places other than Japan. That changed in the early 1980's when new and cheaper methods of growing them were discovered, which allowed for shorter waiting periods between harvests and the ability to cultivate them just about anywhere in the world.

These mushrooms are considered a good choice for the beginner but are not the easiest variety for a first try.

Shiitake mushrooms are an excellent source of Pantothenic Acid, Vitamin B6, Folate, Vitamin D, Magnesium, Manganese, Phosphorus, Potassium, and Zinc.

## Button Mushrooms (Agaricus Bisporus)

Button Mushrooms are known by many other names. Some of them are; common mushroom, table mushroom, white mushroom and several other variations of the above examples.

These mushrooms have been cultivated by people since the 1700's and are the most commonly mushroom grown today. They are used on pizzas, in salads, canned and sold fresh. When you think about eating mushrooms, this is probably the type that comes most readily to mind

In the wild Button, mushrooms can be found growing in open areas such as grassy fields, in the spring or fall after rainstorms. They can be found growing in just about any area of the word.

Button mushrooms are a good variety for novice home growers.

## Enokitake (Flammulina Velutipes)

Another popular mushroom in Asian cuisine, the Enokitake is found growing on Chinese Hackberry tree

and prefer a growing environment rich in carbon dioxide. This mushroom has a long thin stalk and a small cap. Homegrown ones turn out white in color as a result of being grown in the dark. Enokitakes that grow in the wild take on a pinkish hue.

This list is by no means a comprehensive list. There are many types of mushrooms available to you as a small-scale mushroom cultivator. As previously mentioned, Oyster Mushrooms are your best bet, especially while inexperienced.

As you gain experience and become more familiar and comfortable with the process, you will naturally begin to experiment with growing different varieties. Indoor mushroom cultivation becomes more enjoyable and rewarding the more you experience it.

# Ready, Set, GROW!

Growing your first mushroom colony is a three phase project. The first phase involves making sure you have everything you need, the second phase we will talk about the preparations you need to make prior to planting your spawn, and the third phase is growing and enjoying your mushrooms.

First things first, you will need the following gear before you can start setting up your grow area and preparing you spawn:

*A pump bottle or watering can* - You'll want to make sure that you have one that can spray water in the form of a mist. These are easily available in just about any department store. Watering your growing materials and mushrooms with mist in lieu of pouring water directly on them is the correct way to provide your colony with water.

*Growing Trays or containers*- you won't need these if you are using a commercially available growing kit. If you're not, you'll just to find something to place you spawn and growing materials into. Common containers are disposable baking trays, glass jars, a grow bag or even a used gallon jug, such as the kind milk commonly comes in. We will be using an example that utilizes using baking pans, as these are cheap, easy to find and work just fine.

*Basic Gardening Tools* - A set of handheld gardening tools containing a trough, small rake, and a good knife, will always come in handy while growing mushrooms or anything else for that matter. In a pinch, you can get by with a large spoon and a sharp knife.

*Heating pad* - This is used to keep the substrate at the proper temperature during the initial stages of growing.

*Method of sterilization* (depending on the method of growing)–We will be using a microwave oven to sterilize materials for our examples.

*Substrate* - Substrate is the material in which you grow your mushrooms. It is usually a combination of different rooting vegetation and animal waste. Different kinds of mushrooms prefer to grow in different types of materials. If you are using a commercial kit, then you will be provided the correct substrate automatically. If you aren't using a kit, then making the proper substrate could prove both problematic and inconvenient.

Lucky for you, Oyster mushrooms will happily grow in used coffee grounds. Believe it or not, a few pounds of freshly used coffee grounds will provide an almost ideal environment for your Oysters to flourish in. Using used coffee grounds is great for the beginner as it allows you to skip several of the more complicated steps that often deter the newly converted mushroom grower.

*Spawn* - A mushroom spawn is basically any substance that is vaccinated with mushroom mycelium, or the fungus' vegetative stage. It is used to transfer the mycelium to a substrate of the material where the mushrooms would be cultivated. Some of the most common substrates are cardboards, straws, wood chips, and the previously mentioned logs. They come in two different states, live and dried. Stick with the dried as it is more stable, easier to work with and ensures a higher success rate.

The spawn is usually the proper mycelium combined manure and soil and formed into a cake. For best results, you'll want to purchase your spawn from a reputable dealer, either online or from a local supply house.

**Sawdust Spawn**: A sawdust spawn is a sterilized sawdust that has been vaccinated with mushroom mycelium. It is mostly made up of hardwood pieces that are neither too big nor too small, just about a few millimeters in diameter. A sawdust spawn can be used for a variety of other substrates like outdoor mushroom beds, wooden dowels, pasteurized straw, logs, and cardboard.

The advantage of using sawdust as a spawn is that it allows a lot of inoculation points for the mycelium to grow since the sawdust particles are relatively small. This allows the mycelium to colonize in the quickest possible time. However, the downside to using sawdust spawn is that sawdust does not contain much nutrition for the mushroom to grow in. That is why commercially prepared sawdust is enriched with bran and other nitrogen sources to improve yield.

**Grain Spawn**: Grain spawn is made up of sterilized grain that has been vaccinated with a sterile culture of mycelium. Among the types of grain used as spawn are rye, millet, wheat, corn, and other cereal grains. The advantage in using grain spawn is because of the nutritional content it has. This is the most ideal type of spawn for cultivating mushrooms indoor. However, it may be the kind of spawn fitting for outdoor beds because the grain attracts birds and rodents and eats them up.

**Plug Spawn**: Plug spawn is a basically wooden dowels vaccinated with mycelium that are put together. This is best incorporated with sawdust spawn and live mushroom stems. The advantage in preferring a plug dowel is that it's a lot effective for inoculating substrates made up of wood and fibers because it allows the mycelium to colonize wood chips, paper, logs, cardboard, and stumps. However, this may not be fitting for substrates that are made of grain or straw.

**Other Spawn Types**: Mushroom spawn may also come in these forms:

**Woodchip Spawn**: This spawn is made up of wood chips and other varieties of hardwoods.

**Straw Spawn:** This type of spawn is made from pasteurized straw that is vaccinated with mycelium.

**Sawdust Spawn Plugs**: This spawn type is actually a sawdust spawn that is shaped like a plug and has a foam at the end.

**Liquid Spawn:** This is basically a mycelia slurry or water enriched mushroom spores.

It is possible to grow mushrooms from spores, as well as spawn. Using spores is a bit trickier and not recommended.

Once you have everything you need, you'll need to pick a place for your mushroom colony. Remember, you want to mimic as much as possible the way mushrooms grow in the wild.

That means finding a cool, damp part of your house with lighting that you can control. You need to be able to make sure you're mushrooms are kept in a mostly dark atmosphere.

Good spots include basement closets, under sinks, a spare room, etc. Locating a place for you colony shouldn't pose much of a problem.

Large mushroom farms can be very overwhelming for a beginner. For one, it would entail a bigger budget, a larger space to cultivate the mushrooms, and, of course, tons of effort as the person to supervise the processes that unfolds as you start the project. But the good thing about mushroom growing is that they are less complicated than you think. In fact mushroom cultivation, especially of highly prized ones are becoming a trend nowadays.

Mushrooms can be grown through dowels, spawn, and even other growing kits that you can get from your local supplier. These kits come with the instructions and all of the nitty gritty that you need to know. And, what's more, it doesn't require a single equipment.

Whether you want to just supply your own needs or planning to sell mushrooms sooner or later, growing mushrooms at home has a lot of benefits. As food, mushrooms are high in vitamins and nutrients and are low in sodium, calories, and fats. They are also easy to incorporate into a lot of dishes: pasta, stews, soups, etc. So with all these things in mind, you will agree that if you eat mushrooms and want to keep yourself in great form, you might as well try to grow them yourself.

## Example One: Using a Commercially Available Mushroom Growing Kit.

This is the most simple, straightforward way to grow mushrooms. If this is your first try, you really should consider purchasing a kit. They are typically well under fifty dollars and minimize mush of the hassle while maximizing your chances for a successful grow.

There will be detailed instructions that come with your kit, but the basic process is usually along the lines of:

1. Your mushroom kit will consist of everything you need, premixed in a plastic bag. All you need to do is open it.

2. The bag will be placed in a warm, bright area but not on with access to direct sunlight.

3. Mist your bag daily. Make sure you keep the contents of the bag very moist. You need to maintain a fairly humid environment and may want to use a humidifier or place the bag in a plastic tent to ensure proper humidity levels.

4. After a week and a half, the mushrooms will be ready to harvest. The appearance of harvestable mushrooms is called a "flush." The first flush will be the biggest, but your kit may flush more than once, typically two or three times. Harvesting your mushrooms will cause another flush, so don't dilly-dally. Harvest your mushrooms as soon as they are ready to ensure the biggest yield possible. After three months or so you shouldn't expect any more

flushes. This doesn't mean your kit is through growing mushroom for you, though.

5. This step is optional. If you want to squeeze as many mushrooms as possible from your kit, empty the contents somewhere outside. If you have a compost pile or make mulch, try using that spot. You might see another flush or two before the end of the season, as long as environmental factors cooperate.

That's about all there is to growing mushrooms from a kit. It's faster, easier, produces fairly consistent results and is pretty inexpensive compared to the other methods. The only problem with kits is the lack of involvement needed from you. This may or may not be an issue, depending on how much you enjoy the process of growing something. For those of you who want a more complete and hands-on approach to what it is like growing mushroom, you can try your hand with the following method.

## Example Two: Growing Mushrooms Indoors With Coffee Grounds.

Using coffee grounds as a substrate for mushrooms is a little more complicated than a kit, but not as complicated as using other substrates. Because the coffee grounds are already sterilized during the brewing process, you don't have to mess around with sticking odd smelling things into your microwave or pressure cooker. However, you will still find the process more involved and "hands on" than using a kit.

## Getting Ready

To grow mushrooms in coffee you will need:

1. Five to Six pounds of fresh coffee grounds. That's a lot of spent coffee grounds, you need to make sure that there are fresh, i.e., brewed that day.
2. Water Bottle
3. Containers. We will be using a zip lock freezer bag in this example.
4. A mushroom spawn.

When you have gathered your materials, follow these steps:

1. Wash your hands with anti-bacterial soap or use a hand sanitizing lotion to make sure they are nice and clean. You are going to have to mix the spawn into the substrate with your hands and you don't want any microorganisms contaminating your mixture.
2. Place the coffee grinds in the plastic bag. Break up the spawn and mix them together. When you're done, seal the container.
3. Unlike the kit, the coffee ground method requires you place the container in a location that can maintain a temperature of 65–70 degrees F or 20–25 C. It also needs to be dark and humid. After a while, usually three weeks or so, some or of the contents of the bag will appear white. What you are looking at is the

mycelia of your mushroom colony and is a very good sign that things are on track.

4. Cut a hole in the bag and relocate it to an area similar to where you would place a mushroom kit. A warm, humid area with access to indirect light. Water (mist) the bag twice daily and a week later you will see your mushrooms start to appear!

5. As with the kit method, you can expect more than one flush and dispose of the substrate as you would the contents of the kit. You may see even more flushes, depending on the weather.

## Example Three: Growing Mushrooms In Baking Pans.

For this method, you will need everything listed at the top of this chapter. This is the most complicated method we will explain in the book. If you have had success with the first two methods, you may be ready to challenge yourself.

The big differences in this method are that you will need to sterilize your growing materials. You will also have to procure the growing material. You could use coffee grounds, sawdust mixed with coffee grounds or a type of substrate that is specifically suited to your chosen mushroom variety.

## When You Are Ready, Gather Everything You Need And:

1. Sterilize the substrate by putting it in the microwave for two minutes. Place it in

a container, dampen it with water first. After two minutes, the water should have evaporated and you will be left with the sterile substrate.

2. Mix the substrate and the spawn together as you did in method two (also wash your hands for this.). Only this time, do so in the baking pan.

3. Place your pan in a dark place. Just like as in the coffee example. The only difference is that you'll want to place the pan on a heating pad, which has been set to 70 degrees F.

4. From here on out, the procedure is the same as the others. In three weeks or so you will notice the mycelium. Move the pan to a cool, dark area with a temperature between 55 -60 F and cover it with a layer of soil. You should also remove the heating pad. Depending on your area, you might be able to get away with just removing the heating pad and leaving the pan where it is.

5. Water your mushrooms as usual and harvest when ready!

That's all there is to it! If you start with method one and proceed to the more complex methods when you feel ready, soon enough you'll be growing all manner of mushrooms while experimenting with different growing methods. This is a large part of what makes growing your own mushrooms so much fun.

## Example Four: Growing Mushroom In Logs.

Unlike growing plants where one plants seeds, stalk, or branches of the plant, most mushrooms varieties such as shiitake, lion's mane, and oyster mushrooms are supplied are dowels. Wooden dowels are impregnated with mushroom mycelium. The mycelium is actually the vegetative part of the fungus. Then, the mushroom is planted into a log and stored in the fridge or a place where it's cool, dark, and well ventilated. They would stay there until ready for use.

Planting dowels does not require a particular time or season of the year. However, the logs where the mushrooms grow should be cut during the tree's dormant season—

That's somewhere between autumn and spring. The duration required for the dowels to stay planted in the log requires a maximum of 6 weeks after it has been cut. This is put in consideration to avoid contaminating the log with unwanted fungi.

Choose a log that comes from healthy trees in the dormant season. For mushroom growing, it is required to choose logs that are hard, such that of oak, hazel, willow, or birch trees. The diameter of the log should be between 10-15 cms. If you are aiming to support 10-15 dowels, a log with the given diameter must be at least 50 cms in length. To prevent the logs from drying out before use, they must be placed away from strong winds and direct sunlight.

## Planting Dowels

In planting dowels on logs, you need to drill holes and make them 15 cms apart down to the entire length of the log. The rows should have a 7.5 cms intervals around the diameter. Once these holes are drilled, insert the dowels and slightly tap them so that they remain inserted properly and flushed with the log's surface. Then, seal the holes, damaged barks, or cut branch ends with some wax except for the log ends so as to let a little moisture in. Once this is done, you can place the logs in a shady wooded area, or bury them under the ground after wrapping them with a black polyethylene.

See if any cracks appear on the logs. If this happens, soak the log in water for 2 days to wet the bark thoroughly. The process of letting the mushroom mycelium completely colonize the log may take up to 18 months. You will notice this when you see the mycelium begin to appear as a V shape at the log's end. After the log has been fully colonized, you may transfer the log to a moist, warm, and sheltered area to promote fruiting.

Different mushrooms have different required environmental conditions in order to produce fruits. When tiny white nodes begin to appear on the inoculation points on the log, expect to see these nodes grow into mushrooms in a week's time. Remember to keep the humidity and moisture levels at this point, and to keep the log in place.

## Growing Mushrooms Outdoors

Mushrooms can be cultivated and grown outdoors on compost heaps as well as on neglected lawns. Mushrooms love soils that are rich in organic matter. To build a mushroom bed, you'll need to lift a 10-inch pieces of turf and create a depth of about 4 cms, making sure that each square is about 60 cms apart. Then, using a garden fork, loosen the soil beneath the turf squares and add some of your preferred organic matter to make the soil rich. If your soil is poor, it's recommended to use garden compost or some well-rotted manure. Avoid the use of chemical fertilizers as these may not be good in promoting mushroom growth. Once this is done, you can spread the mushroom spawn thinly over the surface of the soil and mix it lightly with the soil. Make sure to keep it just about 1 cms deep. Then, put the turf squares back firmly. Make sure that the soil is kept moist. Note that when cultivating mushrooms outdoors, the weather condition is to be considered as this will dictate the fruiting of the mushrooms.

## Compost

One popular growing medium for growing mushrooms outdoors is by preparing a compost. The traditional method used in preparing a compost is done by mixing hay with animal manure. This type of composting process is encouraged as it allows the propagation of microorganisms that aides in the pre-digestion of the organic materials in the soil will eventually become food for the mycelium.

In the first part of the composting stage, the material is turned and watered every once in a while. By the end of the composting process, the heat caused by the process of decomposition is encouraged to accumulate as this washed away some of the excess ammonia and kills uninvited pests in the soil.

Mushroom composting is used to create a uniform material. However, for larger compost production scales, it would require a continuous flow of raw materials and some handling equipment and the proper know-how. Today, most of the compost facilities are threatened because of our ecology-concerned society when it comes to maintaining an odor-free and pollution free composting production.

## Tips For Harvesting Your Mushrooms

You'll know the mushrooms are ready to harvest when the caps are fully separate from the stems. Think about what opening an umbrella looks like, when your mushrooms look like a fully extended umbrella they are ready to gather.

It is a bad idea to pick you mushrooms out of the ground, instead, twist them from the base until they are separated from the growing material. The easiest way is to cut the base of the stem with a knife.

For mushrooms grown on logs, harvesting is pretty much the same—grabbing the mushroom at the base of the stem and slightly twisting them away from the log. After harvesting, the logs will still continue to grow more fruits until the fourth week. You need to allow some months for the mycelium to recuperate from the harvest and then regenerate. Then, you may produce another crop should you wish to. Note that the same log can still be used and remains productive up to its 6$^{th}$ year.

# Some Other Things You Need To Know About Growing Mushrooms

Cultivating mushrooms could start only as an ordinary hobby. But if you'd like to make a business out of it, why not? If you are considering growing mushrooms for profit, why not invest on oyster mushrooms. Why oyster mushrooms? Oyster mushrooms are the easiest type to grow, and not to mention an exotic type of mushroom. Also, oyster mushroom can grow on just any waste products, straw, woodchips and coffee grounds to name a few.

In growing oyster mushrooms, you will need a dedicated area for growing the mycelium. Someplace where you can control the humidity, the temperature, the light, and other factors that may affect the growth of the mushroom. Also, make sure that your growing area is clean as this will prevent contamination. One way to keep your growing area clean is by following these simple tips:

1. When spreading the pasteurized straw to cool them down, do it in a clean environment. This can be done by washing down and disinfecting the surface to be cooled down.

2. Spray the air in the room with a 10% bleach solution.

3. Make sure to wash your hands diligently before handling the straw spawn and other substances that will be used.

If you'll keep the growing environment clean and make sure your oyster mushrooms are under the right weather conditions, you can expect to harvest oyster mushrooms of a good grade. And don't worry because just in case you are not able to sell them right away, Oyster mushrooms can also be preserved by drying them. Then, you can sell them even months from the time of harvest.

When selling your mushrooms, there are a couple of options:

**At The Local Farmer's Market.** This kind of event is a good avenue for people interested to buy locally produced products to crowd the market and can be a good opportunity for you to get regular consumers even. You can put up a small booth for you to sell your produce.

**Directly To A Local Restaurant.** You can also get regular customers by selling directly to a local restaurant. You may begin negotiating by offering samples of your mushrooms to a local restaurant's chef. Once he approved of the quality of your produce, that restaurant may end up as your regular customer.

**Offering Them To Grocery Stores.** Exotic mushrooms are popular and sellable nowadays. And just like restaurants, if a grocery store would want to buy Oyster mushrooms to sell to people, why would it not be from you? To be specific, try looking at upscale grocery stores whose customers would likely look for exotic mushrooms. What's more, a local grocery store might even give you the opportunity to demonstrate your produce and by doing so, you'll gain more customers for yourself.

**Make Frozen And Pickled Oyster Mushrooms.** If you have a large surplus of your Oyster mushroom harvest that you can't sell right away, another option to make a profit out of it is by making them into pickled mushrooms.

You may consider this pickled mushroom recipe:

You'll need:

- 1 pound fresh Oyster mushrooms, quartered
- 1 tablespoon pepper flakes
- 2 cups water
- 2 cups cider vinegar
- 3 tablespoons garlic, minced
- 2 tablespoons pickling spice
- 1 tablespoon salt

All you need to do is combine the second to the last ingredient and bring it to a boil in a large pot. Then, add in the mushroom. Cook until the mushroom is softened. Then, transfer to a jar. Then, cover and let chill for 10 to 12 hours.

# Why Grow Mushrooms?

A lot of people think that mushroom farming takes great effort and that everyone is up for the task. But if you will into it, mushroom cultivation can be one of those things that you might want to include in your bucket list. It's one of those fun and eye-opening experience that you would not want to miss.

Whatever kind of mushroom you are aiming to raise, or wherever you want to grow it, there would be room to learn something from it. Just as mushrooms enrich the soil, you too will have an enriching experience should you decide to grow mushrooms.

Here are some of the reasons why one must consider growing mushrooms:

**Growing Mushrooms Is Fun.** Just like when planting any other plants, seeing those fungal formations grow and propagate will bring a sense of satisfaction for all your hard work. If you are the type of person you is ever inquisitive and observant of creating and seeing things develop, growing mushrooms just might be the right hobby for you.

**Growing Mushrooms Is Educational.** As was previously mentioned, mushrooms are not plants; they are fungi. And because of that simple fact, it would be impossible to grow mushrooms minus the learning. Cultivating mushrooms will open your mind to the contribution of fungi to the ecosystem. Because they are very different from plants, they require a different way to grow, and that requires for one to dig into the mushroom cycle life. Growing mushrooms is like devoting some quality time to an intricate science project.

**Growing Mushrooms Teaches You To Be More Self-Sufficient.** It's always a joy to grow your own food. Some plant their own vegetables. Others grow herbs in little pots. If you enjoy mushrooms, you don't always have to order in a restaurant or sweep the stalls of your favorite groceries to get some; you can grow them yourself. Wouldn't that be liberating? It gives you such a feeling of self-reliance.

**Growing Mushrooms Will Save You Some Dollars.** If you are thinking about spending for a mushroom kit as something, think of how much more you can save in the long run. Just look at it as an initial investment. Later on, the ROI can even be double, triple or even quadruple of that.

**Growing Mushrooms Are A Sight To See.** Mushrooms are beautiful. There are species that resembles flowers. Some of the mushrooms that are a sight to behold are Reishi, pink oysters, and shiitake mushrooms. If you enjoy looking at flower gardens and meadows, you would also enjoy looking at growing mushrooms.

**Growing Mushrooms Expands Your Sense Of Taste.** When you start to grow mushrooms, you will be very specific about them. You will begin to dig into recipes where each of those edible mushrooms is best with. What's the best dish to include oyster mushrooms? When you grow mushrooms, it will just blow your mind to know about all the sumptuous dishes you can make out of them.

**Growing Mushrooms Allows You To Recycle.** Mushrooms are not difficult to grow. If you have broken pots at home, any old cardboards or used coffee grounds, you can start growing mushrooms on them. This is not only helpful to the environment, but it also takes recycling to a brand new level.

**Growing Mushrooms Sparks Interests.** Everything that we are not used to seeing is fascinating. And because growing mushrooms cannot be compared to planting plants in a pot, it sparks interest and makes us more and more fascinated and curious. And if you are growing mushrooms, what's best than to know the answers to your questions about mushrooms from people who are also into the same hobby. Growing mushrooms is a worthy reason to meet people to share your knowledge with and gather info from.

**Growing Mushrooms Gives You More Superior Ones Than Those Bought Elsewhere.** Mushrooms that are homegrown are always the best. For one, they don't get stressed with the process of traveling from where they are harvested to which supermarket they would be destined to go. If you will look at mushrooms sitting on the shelves of a local grocery, the one that are home grown are always larger, fresher, tastier, and healthier. Growing your mushrooms yourself gives you the assurance that you are getting only organic ones, free from all those chemicals and pesticides that may even impose harm to your health in the long run.

**Growing Mushrooms Open Your Mind To Having A Deeper Appreciation For Nature.** Going mountain climbing, deep sea diving, snorkeling, visiting wondrous sights—all of these activities bring you closer to Mother Nature. That is the same effect that growing mushrooms can give you. You will get to appreciate their beauty, how they thrive in the wild and the mystery of how they grow. When you begin to study them, you will see them more in their natural setting. You will get to see them in a brand new light. If you appreciate the rising and setting of the sun, or the waves as they hit the shore, or the birth of a puppy, or the blossoming of a rose, you will also appreciate how mushrooms grow.

*Mushrooms: A Beginner's guide To Home Cultivation*

# Mushrooms Dishes

## Portobello Mushroom Sauté

For this recipe, you will need:

- 2 Portobello mushroom caps, sliced
- 3 tablespoons olive oil, divided
- 1 ½ tablespoons garlic-flavored olive oil
- ¼ onion, sliced into chunks
- Freshly grated Parmesan cheese
- Freshly grated Asiago cheese
- Salt and pepper, to taste

1. Warm 1 ½ tablespoons olive oil together with 1 ½ tablespoons garlic-flavored olive oil in a skillet using medium heat.
2. Stir in the onions and Portobello mushrooms. Reduce the heat and cook until mushrooms are softened and onions are charred at the edges.
3. Turn off the heat and drizzle remaining 1 ½ tablespoons olive oil.

4. Season with salt and pepper to taste. And sprinkle a generous amount of Parmesan and Asiago cheeses to serve.

## Pho With Mushrooms

For this recipe, you'll need:

1 tablespoon vegetable oil

½ small onion

4 garlic cloves, crushed

1 small ginger, peeled and cut into strips

2 ½ cups beef stock (preferably low-salt)

1 whole star anise

1 cinnamon stick

4 ounces mixed mushrooms (oyster mushroom and shiitake), sliced or torn thinly

1 scallion, sliced thinly

Kosher salt, to taste

2 packages instant ramen (noodles only)

1 ¼ pound beef eye round, sliced crosswise into 1/8" thick

Bean sprouts

Basil leaves

Serrano chilies, sliced thinly

1. In a medium pot, heat some oil set over medium heat. Add in onion, ginger, and garlic.

Stir occasionally for about 4 minutes, until garlic is already golden.
2. Add 1 ½ cups water, beef stock, star anise, and cinnamon. Bring it to a boil.
3. Reduce heat and let simmer for about 8 minutes.
4. Add mushrooms and simmer for another 2 minutes.
5. Add scallion and season with salt to taste.
6. Add beef slices to the soup and let simmer for 20 seconds until cooked through.
7. In another pot, boil ramen until firm to bite. Then, drain the noodles and transfer to bowls.
8. Transfer beef slices to the bowls with noodles and ladle broth into bowls. Garnish with bean sprout, sliced chilies, and basil.

## Pappardelle With Wild Mushrooms

For this recipe, you'll need:

1 ¼ ounces dried porcini mushrooms

12 ounces fresh pappardelle noodles

6 tablespoons unsalted butter

2 tablespoons olive oil

1 shallot minced

½ teaspoons red pepper flakes

1 large Hen of the Woods mushroom (Maitake), trimmed and petals separated (about 3.5 ounces)

1 tablespoon lemon juice

1 tablespoon fresh parsley, chopped (plus more for garnishing)

½ cup grated pecorino cheese

Salt and pepper to taste

1. Add porcini mushrooms in a bowl filled with 2 ½ cups hot water. Set aside for 30 minutes until softened. Drain mushrooms and reserve liquid. Rough chop mushrooms and set aside.
2. Boil a large pot of salted water. Add the pasta and cook as per package instructions.
3. Meanwhile, in a large saucepan, melt butter with olive oil over medium-high heat. Then, add minced shallot and red pepper flakes. Sauté for about 3 minutes until softened.
4. Add the porcini mushroom. Cook for about 3 minutes, stirring occasionally. Then, turn the heat to medium and stir in Maitake mushroom. Stir until tender and coated in butter.
5. Add the lemon juice to the saucepan and ¼ cup of the reserved liquid. Season with salt and pepper to taste.
6. Finally, toss drained pappardelle noodles, mushrooms, and parsley to the pan until

noodles are evenly coated and liquid is absorbed.

7. Serve in bowls and sprinkle with pecorino cheese and parsley.

## Roasted Mushrooms With Butter And Wine

For this recipe, you'll need:

1 pack of crimini mushroom, cleaned, pat dried

4 tablespoons butter, cubed

2 cloves of garlic, minced

¼ cup red wine

2 tablespoons balsamic vinegar

1 tablespoon fresh thyme, minced

Additional thy for garnishing

Salt and pepper to taste

1. Preheat the oven to 450 degrees.
2. Place mushrooms in a baking dish. Then add the wine, balsamic vinegar, thyme, and garlic. Toss them together until the mushrooms are evenly coated.
3. Add some salt and pepper to taste. Then, add the cubed butter.
4. Bake for 15-20 minutes with occasional stirring. See if mushrooms turned golden and are tender, and the liquid is bubbling.

5. Remove from oven and sprinkle with thyme.
6. Serve! This goes perfectly as a side dish to steak or paired with some pasta.

## Creamy Chanterelle Mushroom Soup

For this recipe, you'll need:

1 pound chanterelle mushrooms, cleaned, trimmed, and divided (reserve trimmings)

1 ½ quarts chicken stock (preferably low-salt)

7 tablespoons butter, divided

1 ½ medium shallots, sliced thinly, plus ½ shallot minced

3 medium cloves of garlic, sliced thinly

1 tablespoon flour

1 cup dry sherry (or white wine)

2 bay leaves

6 thyme sprigs, plus ½ teaspoon picked thyme leaves

Kosher salt and ground black pepper to taste

1 tablespoon vegetable oil

1. In a medium saucepan, add mushroom trimmings. Then pour in chicken stock and bring to a boil. Reduce to a simmer and keep warm.
2. In another saucepan set over medium heat, melt 2 tablespoons of butter. Then sauté

## Mushrooms Dishes:

shallots and garlic for 8 minutes, until softened. Add in the mushrooms, reserving only half a cup for garnishing. Cook and stir occasionally for 10 minutes until the liquid evaporates and the mushrooms are cooked through.

3. Add the flour until well incorporated with the mushrooms. Cook for 30 seconds more. Then, pour in dry sherry or white wine. Stir and scrape the bottom of the pan until the liquid has thickened.

4. Using a fine mesh strainer over the soup, pour the broth until all the mushroom scraps are strained. Add bay leaves and thyme sprigs and bring the soup to a simmer for 30 minutes.

5. Transfer the soup to a blender, discarding the thyme and bay leaves. Close with the lid and pulse. Then add four tablespoons of butter one at a time in between pulse, until the butter has been evenly mixed with the soup. Pulse continuously until smooth.

6. Rinse the pot and transfer the soup back, pouring it through a mesh strainer. Season with salt and pepper to taste.

7. Heat some oil in a medium saucepan set over high heat until smoky. Add in reserved mushrooms and toss continuously until browned. Add mince shallots and thyme. Cook for about 15 seconds until fragrant. Add 2 tablespoons of water and what's left of the

butter. Remove pan from heat and season with salt and pepper to taste.

8. Finally, ladle soup into warm bowls and add sautéed mushroom mixture on top. Serve!

# Conclusion

Thank you again for purchasing this book!

I hope this book was able to help you to better understand the process of growing mushrooms indoors for food and fun.

The next step is to choose a mushroom type to grow and gather your supplies. After that, pick a method for growing and get started.!

Finally, if you enjoyed this book, please take the time to share your thoughts and post a review on Amazon. It'll be greatly appreciated!

Thank you and good luck!

Ben

# Other Related Books

Below you'll find some other popular books that are available on Amazon and Kindle as well. Simply type the url into your favorite browser to check them out!

**An Introduction To Home Mushroom Cultivation**

http://www.amazon.com/dp/B00OYK43WS

## Mushrooms 101: A Beginner's Guide to Growing Mushrooms at Home

## http://www.amazon.com/dp/B00SDHLCAO

If the links do not work, for whatever reason, you can simply search for these titles on the Amazon website to find them.

# Photo Credits

All photographs used in the book were provided free for commercial use with no attribution required from www.pixabay.com

License: CCo Public Domain / FAQ

https://pixabay.com/en/service/terms/#usage

Printed in Great Britain
by Amazon